Erica Gonçalves
Soraia Mello

Cyberculture, feminism and gender issues in education

Erica Gonçalves
Soraia Mello

Cyberculture, feminism and gender issues in education

ScienciaScripts

Imprint

Cover image: www.ingimage.com

This book is a translation from the original published under ISBN 978-620-2-04000-6.

Publisher:
Sciencia Scripts
is a trademark of
Dodo Books Indian Ocean Ltd. and OmniScriptum S.R.L publishing group

120 High Road, East Finchley, London, N2 9ED, United Kingdom
Str. Armeneasca 28/1, office 1, Chisinau MD-2012, Republic of Moldova, Europe
Managing Directors: Ieva Konstantinova, Victoria Ursu
info@omniscriptum.com

Printed at: see last page
ISBN: 978-620-8-40701-8

To Tito Sena who shines, inspires and remains on the path of education and feminism...

ACKNOWLEDGMENTS

Thank you to the entire GDE (Gender and Diversity at School) team who welcomed us, encouraged us and were by our side the whole time. There are many names who have passed through and left us flowers, thoughts and reflections and this sheet or even a whole notebook would not be enough to record the incredible people we have met throughout the course.

My special thanks go to my teacher and friend Tito Sena (in memorian) and my teacher and friend Tania Welter, who sparked my interest in gender and sexuality issues, especially at school.

I would also like to thank my friends and partners: Jessica Viana and Juliana Andozio. And new friends Cali Castro, Gisele de Mozzi and Luciana Gerent.

Professors Olga Regina Garcia and Miriam Grossi for their inspiration, determination and for believing that we can take great feminist steps towards human rights.

To my advisor, Soraia Carolina de Mello, for her patience, care and guidance, without altering the paths of thought, in the light of gender and diversity.

I would like to express my special thanks for the funding given to the Specialization in Gender and Diversity at School at the Federal University Santa Catarina (GDE/UFSC) through the National Fund for the Development of Education (FNDE) managed by SECADI/MEC (Secretariat for Continuing Education, Literacy, Diversity and Inclusion of the Ministry of Education) during the administration of President Dilma Rousseff (2011-2015), without which it would have been impossible to carry out a two-year course in five cities in different regions of the state of Santa Catarina. Above all, we would like to thank for the investments that over the last 13 years have made it possible to expand public policies to combat hunger, racism, sexism, lesbophobia, homophobia, transphobia and ableism. Unfortunately, the political situation over the last year has almost made it impossible to complete this third edition of the GDE, especially after the abolition of SECADI, which was created in 2004 and which made it possible to hold hundreds of courses on the themes of differences, inequalities and human rights throughout Brazil. It was a government policy that unfortunately did not become a state policy; on the contrary, it has been extinguished and criminalized by various conservative sectors in society. May this specialization be remembered as a space of resistance and struggle for a fairer and more equal society.

I began to understand that the pen [digital technologies] and words can be much more powerful than machine guns, tanks or helicopters. We were learning to fight. And to realize how powerful we are when we speak out. Malala Yousafzai, 2015, p.167

SUMMARY

Discussions of gender and feminism are present in different discourses and can be expanded with cyberculture. In this text, therefore, the aim is to present how the feminist and human rights discourse is materialized in the voice of the young Pakistani activist Malala Yousafzai, whether through the dissemination in the news represented by digital information and communication technologies (DICTs) or through (printed) children's story books. All of these media channels are part of a set of actors that contribute to integrating feminism in a more participatory way as a movement fighting for human rights. Thus, this bibliographic and qualitative study uses books, articles and videos as research sources to problematize feminism as a movement to be gestated within institutions such as schools, the media and the home itself. Although not exactly a finished result, this analysis of the content investigated points to a perspective of continuity, partnership and motivation for demands mediated by stories of real women fighting for equal rights and the suppression of the gender hierarchy and inequalities.

Keywords: Malala Yousafzai. Digital media. Children's stories. Cyberculture. Feminism.

SUMMARY

1 INTRODUCTION

Children's literature can be considered an important vehicle for disseminating themes related to scientific and conceptual education on different subjects. In this study, we prioritize the approach to gender as a feminist movement of resistance and struggle for equity. In favor of human rights in today's society, whether proclaimed by the media in the most varied forms, children's and young adult literature can help in the understanding and appropriation of possibilities for perceiving the world from an early age.

Faced with this playful scenario, which at the same time raises awareness and problematizes gender issues as human rights, we seek to move between three bases of support: cyberculture, children's literature and feminism. These three themes form the confluence for the star of this academic and scientific stage: Malala Yousafzai. A young Pakistani woman who won the Nobel Peace Prize in 2014 for demanding the right of girls to go to school after the Taliban regime invaded her hometown in the Swat Valley (Pakistan).

To compose this investigation, we invited reference theorists who dialog with each other and strengthen the feminist and cyberculture arguments present in the text. We therefore highlight Donna Haraway (2009) in particular, with her metaphor of the cyborg as an element of fiction and reality that critically relates to the world in order to think about and reflect on the politics of this century, and Bruno Latour (2012), who contributes to understanding the cyborg as an actor, i.e. a human or non-human element (digital technologies, for example) that promotes some action or modification in the context.

In this circuit to understand the feminist cybernetic movement of today's society, other names have helped us to reflect: Judith Butler (2003) and Guacira Louro (2003) to understand the notion of gender; Stig Hjarvard (2012/2015) the concept of mediatization; Ismar Soares (2014) educommunication and Jesus Martin-Barbero (2014) the characterization of communicative ecosystems.

Between printed material (books) and audiovisual material (DVD - Digital Versatile Disk), the biography of the protagonist of this study, whether through children's literature, the documentary via DVD or, above all, Malala's autobiography, presents us with one of many stories of women fighting for human rights and gender equality. Thus, we have developed three chapters which, although they can be read at random due to their independent nature, are carefully embroidered in dense threads that unite around a set of issues to be thought about and debated in relation to gender and feminism.

The chapter "FROM FAIRY TALES TO THE NOBEL PEACE PRIZE: children's literature, feminist history and social movements" discusses the process of mediatization that places us in a heteronormative, white and submissive world in cold, distant castles and imposes stereotyped standards of how to be, live and think. The turning point in the game of powers and possibilities comes when a book of children's literature, such as Malala by Adriana Carranca (2015), breaks with this stereotype of idealized fairytale children's literature and offers the life story of a real character who changed the paradigms of her time: winner of the Nobel Peace Prize in 2014.

In "EDUCOMMUNICATIVE CYBORGES: FEMINISM IN CYBERCULTURE", we seek to bring digital media to the center of the dialogue as an important actor in breaking down heteronormative stereotypes and raising awareness of the political importance of feminism with Donna Haraway's (2009) metaphor of the cyborg. These augurs, as practices
(SOARES, 2014) can also promote new objectives for education, especially by transforming the instrumental vision of digital technologies into mediators of the teaching and learning process, linked to the feminist movement. By establishing

social relationships that respect differences and are based on a flat and symmetrical ontology, as Latour (2012) presents with Actor-Network Theory (ANT), the stories of real women who have contributed in some way to reducing gender hierarchies are presented as strategies that enhance pedagogical dialogue, such as the inspiring story of Malala Yousafzai.

Last but not least, the title "MALALA'S VOICE THROUGH DIGITAL MEDIA: THE RIGHT TO GO TO SCHOOL" problematizes Malala's story as a human rights defender fighting to ensure that Pakistani girls and girls from all societies go to school. Under the pseudonym Gul Makai, Malala reveals to the world what was happening in the Swat Valley with the Taliban invasion and this story doesn't end here. It continues with the strength and determination of people who fight and write the stories of humanity. This title, therefore, reinforces the visibility of the history of women who claim rights and directly confront regimes of gender hierarchy, under the digital means of information and communication.

2 FROM FAIRY TALES TO THE NOBEL PEACE PRIZE: children's literature, feminist history and social movements

Fairy tales seem to be among the most popular literary genres for children and young adults. These narratives are part of the human imagination and permeate the universe of imagination, fantasy, consumption and the reproduction of naturalized stereotypes of female fragility and submission. In order to understand the process that is part of this movement that integrates imagination with reality, we sought support from Stig Hjarvard's (2012; 2015) concept of mediatization. This author discusses the central place that the media occupy in everyday experiences and how they trigger actions and mediations that we are often unaware of. As an example: when watching a film about idealized princesses, a child, perhaps even an adult, wants to experience the cinematic episodes by buying a backpack with that character's image on it, or even wants to "be" the princess, looking for her main characteristics, including the phenotypical ones: long hair, white, thin.... In these cases, it's possible that the interlocutor will feel low self-esteem and devalued because they don't fit into the standards designed and naturalized by advertising and propaganda.

Storytelling is part of memory and the recording of facts, events and imagination. From oral tradition to the latest digital technological resources, stories remain at the media level materialized by children's and young adult books.

[...] people have always been interested in storytelling. They enjoy movies, television soap operas or novels because, fundamentally, these genres tell a story. When these means of communication didn't yet exist, it was family and community gatherings - the first manifestations - that took on this role. There are several conditions that can give rise to our particular interest in stories. Firstly, the fact that life itself can be understood as a story - a succession of events and emotions. Another reason, which perhaps justifies this passion, is the identification with the feelings of the characters (PIRES, 2009, p. 85-86).

In continuity with these fairytale narratives, especially as they are part of society as a pedagogical and social institution, it is necessary to take into account that the school is inserted in this mediatized context in which teachers, children, families consume, produce and move the market of children's and young adult literature that materialize the gender issues immersed in the contents of traditional fairytales such as **Snow White, Cinderella, Sleeping Beauty,** among others.

However, we mustn't forget that these and other fairy tales are part of the representation of the child's imagination and cognitive development. Thus,

> [...] fairy tales fascinate children because of their stories and represent, according to Marilena Chaui (1984), a wealth and multiplicity of meanings, seducing different areas of knowledge such as literature, philosophy, history, sociology, psychology, psychoanalysis, etc. Various authors have discussed the importance of children being in contact with fairy tales [...] Fairy tales have a structure that is easily understood and therefore make listening or reading pleasurable. In this type of reading, the child has fun, creates fantasies, because the tales talk about fears, love, the difficulties of being a child, needs and self-discovery. (BASTOS; NOGUEIRA, 2016, p.15-16)

Recent publications by contemporary authors such as Edgar Kirchof, Tatiana Bonin and Rosa Maria Silveira (2013), Suyan Pires (2009) and Rodolpho Bastos and Joanna Nogueira (2016), seek to discuss in their articles precisely this role of reproducing feminine and masculine behaviors and stereotypes coming from these narratives represented by children's literature.

In view of the need to rethink the gender roles that legitimize women's submissive place in society, these authors, among others, propose a critical reading of fairy tales from different perspectives: power relations, family arrangements, differences (cultural, phenotypical, intellectual).

Chaui (1984) points to Sleeping Beauty as another example, in which the woman waits to be awakened, socially and sexually, by the male figure, or rather, Prince Charming. Stories like Snow White and The Little Mermaid also reproduce this ideal of female happiness reduced to finding the perfect husband, always featuring docile, patient and coy heroines, and villages envious of their beauty (physical beauty in the first case, and the beautiful voice of the mermaid protagonist Ariel in the second). Once we understand how gender stereotypes are presented and reinforced in traditional fairy tales, which are the fruit of a patriarchal culture in which women need rescuing and men are given the task of being saviors, [...] we can use these stories in the classroom, not to perpetuate, but to problematize and rethink these established social roles. (BASTOS; NOGUEIRA, 2016, p. 22)

In other words, a large part of children's literature prioritizes the idealized love of marriage, the difficulty of conquering it and the feeling of transforming the other. Thus, according to Suyan Pires (2009, p. 86), literary works can be interpreted as cultural artifacts that legitimize "social and gender identities, establish power relations between the sexes and the sexes". readers and writers of such texts, constituting a producing and reproducing circuit of masculine and feminine social practices considered ideal."

With this in mind, it is necessary to highlight the category of gender, which is based especially on the studies of Judith Butler (2003), Guacira Lopes Louro (2003) and Joan Scott (1990). While Scott (1990) uses gender to explain the differences between men and women based on the social relationships constructed in discourse in different historical contexts; for Louro (2003), the differences between men and women are not only represented in the body - penis or vagina - but there is also a cultural component which is evident in clothing, behavior and ways of thinking and acting. Judith Butler (2003), for her part, reiterates the criticism of the representation of gender roles and questions the dualism of male/female, female/male polarized in society and culturally constructed.

Whether we like it or not, these gender-based discourses are so strongly entrenched in different spheres of everyday life (in films, books, domestic relations, family hierarchy, jobs...) that children and adults, throughout the learning process, assimilate and incorporate them as subjective elements of the essence of human nature. Thus, "We come to live with situations that are often perceived as natural, but which have been constructed and continue to be legitimized as social practices." (PIRES, 2009, p. 83)

However, if we think that this nature is the product of a social and historical construction, it is possible to reflect on and question these fixed gender roles within hierarchies of power and domination, starting with one of the most influential and participatory institutions in our society: the school.

Rodolpho Bastos and Joanna Nogueira (2016) state that fairy tales not only reinforce gender roles, but also add to these roles dichotomous values of good/evil, ugly/beautiful, hero/villain, good guy/bad guy, princess/witch. This polarized construction, which Judith Butler (2003) criticizes, can be problematized at school by education professionals by using fairy tales from other perspectives, especially those of gender and diversity in the historical and social context. Thus,

> [...] clarifying the origin of the narratives is one of the alternatives that the teacher can find to explain and think about why all the central characters are represented in the same way: male/dominator and female/dominated, evil witch/mistress and good princess, prince savior and princess to be rescued, as well as the idea that a happy ending is always linked to a wedding. This approach makes it possible to demonstrate why the same characters are physically and historically represented by people who are not part of the pupil's reality, thus encouraging reflection on current social roles. (BASTOS; NOGUEIRA, 2016, p. 24)

In view of the above, we believe that the dialogue on gender issues can be initiated especially in the school environment, from the first years of basic education, where children already have contact with different types of literature even before they are literate, through literacy in different languages (audiovisual, digital, symbolic).

In this sense, women's history itself provides diverse examples that do not correspond to the stereotypes of Western fairy tales, and that different models of femininity can be accessed through these stories. Thus, the question posed by this research is: how can knowledge of women's history be used to consolidate the debate on girls' empowerment, especially at school?

The answer may lie in the historical children's literature itself, which deals with the life and legacy of a Pakistani girl called Malala Yousafzai, who found in digital media a way to fight for and demand the right of women to go to school and study. Thus, the object of this study is an educational tool, the book "Malala, the girl who wanted to go to school", in which the author turns to the children's audience and discusses the life of a real character who changed the paradigms of her time: Malala Yousafzai, winner of the Nobel Peace Prize in 2014 (CARRANCA, 2015).

Figure 1 - Cover of the children's book Malala. Source: Carranca, 2015

Based on the premise that the media are part of people's daily social and cultural lives, this study is based on the hypothesis that Malala Yousafzai's story can contribute to consolidating knowledge of gender and diversity issues at school. Thus, by problematizing the actions of this young Pakistani activist from the first stage of Basic Education , an institutional school process of mediatization begins that can alter, modify and produce other ways of thinking, acting and feeling in children. And, especially with the digital information and communication technologies available in contemporary society, the Nobel Peace Prize winner (2014) can be recognized worldwide for having broken with cultural and social patterns, building new paradigms in today's society.

> Malala was a girl who wanted to go to school. But where she lived, this was forbidden. Books were hidden. On the way to school there were many dangers. Unimaginable risks, even death. This place is called the Swat Valley. The Swat Valley is in a faraway country called Pakistan. It has green fields, surrounded by giant mountains that the snow paints white almost all year round. In summer, when the sun warms the peaks, the snow melts and joins the Swat River, which winds its way down the mountain to meet the Kabul River, which comes from neighboring Afghanistan. There, between the magnificent Hindu Kush mountain range and the crystal-clear waters of the rivers, with one foot in Pakistan and the other in Afghanistan, the Pashtuns, like Malala, have lived for over 2,000 years. (CARRANCA, 2015, p. 9)

In this study, we believe that it is important that, along with the narrative of any story, the historical, cultural and temporal context of its characters is placed, highlighting the roles of men and women in different cultures and societies. The main aim of this research is therefore to problematize the transformative potential of historical knowledge and the importance of digital media in the fight for gender issues and the empowerment of girls through children's literature.

Social relations and cultural differences are present at all times in Adriana Carranca's book (2015). In the following excerpt, the author discusses these differences, which she noticed while visiting the land where Malala was born, the Swat valley in Pakistan.

After breakfast, the boys went out to play. Using tree branches as swords, they would fight for dominance of the tiny space in the yard. The girls didn't have much time for this because they helped their mothers with the housework. Only Tanzeela, aged four, still didn't wear a veil and enjoyed the perks of playing with the boys. Aimun, fourteen, was the oldest and the quietest. She looked like a sad little girl. Razia told me that she and her husband had already received three marriage proposals for their daughter, because the girls in the valley get married very early. Razia is illiterate and married Sana when she was fifteen. But Aimum didn't want to marry young, like her mother. Like Malala, she wanted to go to school. (CARRANCA, 2015, p. 27)

This excerpt contains different types of perceptions of gender and cultural differences. It is important to note that in recent years, according to the authors Edgar Kirchof, Tatiana Bonin and Rosa Maria Silveira (2013), there has been a significant increase in interest in issues related to differences, especially in cultural artifacts aimed at children. This phenomenon may be related to current public policies on the recognition and rights of differences, whether cultural, social, phenotypical or otherwise.

Among these, children's literature has emerged as a fertile field for the thematization of ethnic, age, racial, disability, sexual orientation, gender and body conformation differences, given the almost consensual conception - among educators - that approaching themes through cultural entertainment products such as children's literature books, films, cartoons and games is always productive and fruitful. [...] There are many factors that have contributed and continue to contribute to the centrality of the issue of differences today, including, on the one hand, the initiatives of political movements and a range of new social actors demanding specific rights - many of which have been incorporated into legislation based on the constitutional premise of equality and, at the same time, respect for cultural, religious, ethnic and generational differences, etc. On the other hand, it is necessary to consider, in addition to the social and political factors of the Brazilian state, the ongoing processes of globalization, which make the borders that delimit an inside and an outside increasingly porous, which define who is close or distant, who we are and who the others are, and significantly alter the cultural panoramas, routines and practices of the subjects of these times. (KIRCHOF; BONIN E SILVEIRA, 2013, p. 1045)

Although there is a good amount of scientific production on children's literature and fairy tales problematized from a gender perspective, the justification for this study is based on the lack of articles both on the Scielo platform[1] (Scientific Electronic Library Online) containing the name "Malala" in the abstract, subject and title, and in the search for works with the keyword "Malala" in the Digital Library of Theses and Dissertations of the Brazilian Institute of Information on Science and Technology (BDTD IBICT)[2] . In this sense, we noticed a gap in this area of research, which we have developed here through the figure of one of the youngest female Nobel Peace Prize winners in history.

As a contribution to the advancement of education in gender and human rights, we hope that this research can provide pedagogues and teachers with tools for an education in gender and diversity at school from a feminist and inclusive perspective of valuing ethno-racial, gender and social differences. Inspired by the stories of real women who took part in social movements to fight for and demand rights for reasons that go beyond fairy tales (where the dream is to marry a prince and live happily ever after), in this study we are interested in problematizing the transformative potential from the point of view of the confluence of historical knowledge and the importance of digital media in the fight for gender issues and the empowerment of girls supported by children's literature. As a result of this movement, we hope to contribute to the knowledge of gender and diversity issues at school based on children's books for the early years of elementary school.

By embracing the idea that children's literature can be an important

[1] For more information, visit http://www.scielo.org

[2] To find out more, visit http://bdtd.ibict.br/

educational tool and pedagogical device for learning about women's history, the paths to achieving this level of equal rights are outlined in particular by presenting and publicizing one of the possibilities for feminist social struggles and movements in cyberspace, bringing to light the life story of Pakistani activist Malala Yousafzai. In the course of the book, the author describes the moment when the Taliban occupied the Swat Valley in Pakistan and ordered that schools be closed and computers destroyed. At this time, Malala and her father started a campaign that would change the history of women and digital social movements,

> Malala knew that it says in the Heart that everyone should seek knowledge. So she remembered how important it is to know letters and books. Like the poet Khushal, after whom the school is named, she made words her weapon. "My strength is not in my sword. It's in the pen," she said one day. Malala started writing a blog!
> For safety's sake, she chose a pseudonym: Gul Makai, a heroine of Pashtun folklore, who in Malala's language gives her name to a beautiful blue flower. Gul Makai's blog was published in Urdu on the website of the BBC radio and television network, in Britain, the Queen's homeland. Malala wrote with surprising refinement for a tribal girl, which helped draw attention to the problems of the valley. [...]
> Malala's story, written for a children's audience, leaves no stone unturned when it tells of the strength and determination of Malala, a girl from a very distant place, full of barriers and dangers, but who, through digital social networks, managed to tell the world about the cruelties happening in her region. Girls' education was still banned and Malala was saddened to see her uniform, backpack and geometry kit in the corner, unused. She missed school and even the discussions with her classmates. But the Taliba had ordered the girls not to leave. For months, they were trapped inside the house. Malala wrote everything on her blog, where she could be free. It also became the only place where outsiders could observe what was happening in the valley, like peeking through a keyhole. The events reported shocked people in other parts of Pakistan and the world. Malala gained many readers and everyone commented on what she wrote [...] (CARRANCA, 2015, p. 46-47; 49)

Malala was attacked by a Taliban group and spent five months in a hospital in England, where she had to move because of the danger she was in of being attacked by fundamentalists. With this, Malala stands out for her courage, boldness and strategy in defending women's rights, especially the right to go to school.

> Her fight for girls' education has gained global attention and thousands of people have joined her. Malala has received donations to help millions of girls and boys who are still out of school. She made the list of the hundred most influential people in the world and became the youngest ever Nobel Peace Prize winner! [...]
>
> - I've realized a dream. I think it's the happiest moment of my life because I'm going back to school. Today I have my books, my backpack, and I'm going to learn... I want to learn about politics, about social rights and about the law. I want to learn about how I can change the world - she said, on the first day of school. The first day of the rest of her life." (CARRANCA, 2015, p. 80)

Thus ends the fairy tale about a real girl who fought and still fights for women's rights. Malala tells us that the ending can be a happy one, all we have to do is break away from the bonds of prejudice, violence and gender differences. Each of us can idealize a Malala as a representation of strength and overcoming.

The aim of this children's story was to promote reflection on the issues of gender, self-esteem and female representation that permeate the media universe in the educational sphere. The aim of this study is to provide tools for teachers and pedagogues, especially in the early stages of basic education, in order to contribute to gender and diversity education at school from a feminist and inclusive perspective of valuing ethno-racial, religious, gender and social differences.

3 EDUCOMMUNICATIVE CYBORGS: FEMINISM IN CYBERCULTURE

Cyberculture has a direct relationship with creative capacity and technological materialization in the social and historical context. It is in this context of transformation that digital media influence and are influenced by social and feminist movements. It is in this vein of thought that Donna Haraway (2009) chooses the figure of the cyborg, a character who appears in science fiction stories, to claim values and political appropriations of differences and feminism concomitant with the scientific and technological development that contemporary society has experienced.

In other words, Haraway's "Cyborg Manifesto" (2009) is a political proposal for transforming our perception of the world and ourselves, guided by our social relationships experienced at the turn of the century/millennium and through cyberculture.

> Cyberculture is the historical moment, the everyday dialectical connection between social subjects and their technological expressions, through which we transform the world and thus our own inner and material way of being in a given direction (RUDIGER, 2013, p.112-113).

With the advent of digital technologies and cyberculture, the boundaries between the organic and the inorganic, human and non-human (LATOUR, 2012) are narrowing and the division between Nature and Society is being questioned by contemporary authors and sociology scholars such as Bruno Latour (2012) and Donna Haraway (2009).

Figure 3 - Donna Haraway.
Source: Google Images

Figure 4 - Bruno Latour.
Source: Google

These transformations are also taking place in the physical and natural sciences with the new paradigms of science proposed by Relativistic Mechanics and Quantum Mechanics (ROVELLI, 2015). This contemporary society, which experiences uncertainty and relativity mainly in the erasure of the division between the visible and the non-visible, matter and energy, is now looking for other ways of understanding life and social relations.

In Donna Haraway's (2009) interpretation of what this cyborg is, it is the very break with the forms of control and power that have long maintained their ideological domination of the bodies and minds of men and women. Thus, this hybrid of human and machine that promotes axes and associations, referred to by Latour (2012) as an actant, can help us to

> [...] transforming in a liberating sense our experiences with our culture, our work, our way of life, our social relations and our individual identities. The predomination of what he calls the informatics of domination does not exclude the possibility of using new technologies to change the rules of the game, to bring about new pleasures, social situations and power relations (RUDIGER, 2013, p.117).

In this sense, Donna Haraway (2009) proposes a break with the categories - among them, that of "woman", in a naturalized way. This single identity, with the metaphor of the cyborg, can be replaced by new politics of identification within a symmetry of men and women, machines and humans, nature and society, which Latour (2012) calls flat ontology (LATOUR, 2012). Thus,

> [...] the cyborg is a historical figure with which to construct and alter the mixture of human beings and machines in which, little by little, through this very ambivalence, we have been converting since the end of the 20th century. Today 'the machine has lost its status as something to be animated, worshipped or dominated. The machine is now us, something that structures us, an aspect of our incarnation. We must be responsible for the machines: they don't dominate or threaten us. We are responsible for the limits: we are the same as them and, therefore, they are something subject to construction and deconstruction, a terrain where our identity has come to be disputed, a field where, contradictorily,

it is true, we are gaining access to a new way of looking at science and technology and, potentially, questioning the informatics of domination. (RUDIGER, 2013, p.117-118)

For Haraway (2009), therefore, both the male/female dualism characteristic of gender discourse and that of nature/society contribute to the fragmentation and partiality of science, technology and society (STS). In other words, within the new perspective of social relations - in a network or web - in a continuous state of association and modification, which is based on Latour (2012) and Haraway (2009), among others, dualism translates into a contradictory process. It is because of this complexification of social relations, which are increasingly driven by the mediation of science and technology, that Donna Haraway (2009) presents the cyborg as an element of fiction and reality that critically relates to science, technology and society (STS) in order to think and reflect on integrated policies in this new century.

A cyborg is a cybernetic organism, a hybrid of machine and organism, a creature of social reality and also a creature of fiction. Social reality means lived social relations, it means our most important political construction, it means a fiction capable of changing the world. International women's movements have constructed what can be called the " women's experience". This experience is both a fiction and a fact of the most crucial, political kind. Liberation depends on building awareness of oppression, on its imaginative apprehension and, therefore, on awareness and apprehension of possibility. The cyborg is the stuff of fiction and also of lived experience - an experience that changes what counts as female experience at the end of the 20th century. It's a life-and-death struggle, but the boundary between science fiction and social reality is an optical illusion. (HARAWAY, 2009, p.36)

Based on this premise, Haraway's Cyborg Manifesto (2009) provides an overview of the influence of media and communication advances on the social and cultural practices of contemporary networked society by bringing political activism within digital technologies to areas such as the discussion of feminism, gender, power and diversity. However, for Francisco Rudiger (2013, p.126-127)

> Networked life takes its political toll on us by positioning us in circuits of interaction which, as well as being ephemeral, fractionated and functional, tend to be activated or remain only in the abstract, anonymous and (audio)visual register of technological devices. The subject, it is true, is only reduced to the connections he establishes on social networks as an ideology, but this does not mean that the process is not underway and, with it, a world is projected in which there is no longer any place for both the living and creative relationship with his fellow man and for the collaborative and concrete construction of consciously revolutionary institutions.

The change in society's way of thinking and acting with the advent of technology did not begin with this digital format. Other technological inventions and processes long before digital forms of technology were responsible for these changes in social relations. Derrick Kerckhove (2009, p.43) states that "Developed and perfected over five millennia, the alphabet became the most important concept, occupying the mind, soul and body of every human culture until the discovery of electricity". In other words, after writing, because we live in a graphocentric society, electricity, as well as our dependence on it, exemplifies this current paradigm immersed in the culture of contemporary society. With the advent of electricity, therefore, the way of living and thinking were altered and modified, establishing needs and driving other scientific and technological developments until the arrival of the digital world.

In this continuum, connected to cyberspace via the internet and satellite signals, computers transcend geographical boundaries and integrate a wide network of relationships between human and non-human elements (LATOUR, 2012), through cyberculture. The internet is linked to the practices and actions of people who, when traveling through cyberspace, interact with selected content and promote the "constant exchange of knowledge that circulates, is modified, reconstructed, augmented and edited according to the specific demands of a given situation" (MARTINO, 2015. p.31). This circuit communication is intertwined with cyborgs in these relationships and associations between science, technology and society (STS). Therefore, for Haraway (2009, p. 37),

> The cyborg is our ontology; it determines our politics. The cyborg is a condensed image of both imagination and material reality: these two centers, combined, structure any possibility of historical transformation.

The strong presence and influence of technologies, especially digital ones, changes the relationships established in the social and cultural spheres, which are also present in social movements, especially feminism, whose logic of thought, consumption and action is the same when it comes to people who live in this current space and time. A strong example of this is Malala Yousafzai, who told the world about the daily life of the Pakistani people when the Taliban took over and prevented girls from going to school. With this in mind, it is possible to think of different forms and situations of political demands through digital media - cyborgs.

The metaphor of the cyborg can be thought of as a strong contribution to a feminist culture "in the utopian tradition of imagining a world without gender, which will perhaps be a world without genesis, but perhaps also a world without an end". (HARAWAY, 2009, p.38) The author also characterizes the figure of the cyborg as a being without gender (post-gender) that moves away from the polarized condition of a sexuality divided between homo and hetero. To illustrate this, Donna Haraway (2009) takes up fictional stories and argues that the cyborg doesn't expect his creator father to build a heterosexual partner to complement him, after all, "the cyborg doesn't dream of a community based on the model of the organic family" (ibdem, p.39).

And what does all this have to do with teaching and learning in schools? Who are these subjects of history who share the same experiences with cyborgs? And how can we think of an education that goes beyond the dichotomous and dualistic barrier that separates and hierarchizes men and women?

The role of educating is not just that of the school as a teaching institution, but of this network of humans and non-humans who make up the social networks in a two-way process in which they are both receivers and producers of information content. In other words, under the same hybrid horizon are children and teachers, prejudices and dualisms, hopes and digital technologies.

It is in this context that Nelson Pretto (2013) points out that both teachers and children are immersed in a digital culture of information and communication. This makes it necessary and urgent to reflect on the role of education and schooling in this media and mediatized context, especially in overcoming situations of gender discrimination and hierarchy.

School is no longer the only place where knowledge is constructed and reconstructed. Faced with immense channels through which information is accessed, exchanged and discussed beyond the walls of the school, there has been a paradigm shift in education, which is no longer conceived as being centered on teaching but is now based on collaboration and collective construction, instigated by technological development (SARTORI, 2014, p.68).

Based on the discussion of the role of the media in educational processes to break down prejudices and raise awareness of the political importance of feminism, new objectives for education are being identified. In view of the study of communicative and educational actions, relationships and associations, as well as the growing importance that the media and the development of technologies are acquiring in social relationships, interfering in the production of knowledge and culture. In this logic, with the emergence of new communicative practices, perhaps not so new since they began at the end of the last millennium, and with the advancement of digital technologies, other pedagogical practices can be thought of and implemented.

In this sense, Educommunication has become a new area of knowledge that seeks to meet the demands present in schools, seeking to unravel the communicative processes generated in the educational environment that interfere in students' learning processes and their development with the influence of media technologies. (SARTORI, 2014, p.116)

Educommunication, as Ismar Soares (2014) argues, an area of knowledge delineated from the approximation between Communication and Education - communicating in education and educating in communication, requires another way of thinking about pedagogical models and educational strategies that can promote and facilitate dialogue between the subjects that make up the school community in a critical, collective, creative and democratic way. And if contemporaneity, immersed in the technological and mediatized context, modifies and alters ways of thinking, acting and living, it is also necessary to discuss different ways of teaching and learning in the school sphere, based on the political logic of these new feminisms that emerge as cyborgs of contemporary society.

For generations, women have been told that they are "naturally" weak, submissive, extremely emotional and incapable of abstract thought. That it was "in their nature" to be mothers rather than executives, that they would rather entertain guests at home than study particle physics. If all these things are so natural, they can't be changed. End of story. Back to the kitchen. No further action.

On the other hand, if women (and men) are not natural, but constructed, like a cyborg, then given the right tools, we can all be reconstructed. Everything can be chosen, from washing the dishes to legislating on the Constitution. (KUNZRU, 2016, p.25)

In this sense, the cyborg metaphor contributes to thinking about school education as a field of communicative pedagogical practices articulated in networks and which go beyond the dichotomized boundaries between humans (children, teachers, school community) and non-humans (digital technologies, machines). In other words, the field of educommunication denotes a less formalist sense of education with the possibility of thinking, reflecting and problematizing, together with the children and the school community, the constitution of policies based on principles of diversity and respect. Haraway's (2009) feminist approach , which breaks down the dichotomous and hierarchical barrier of gender, can be an inspiration for establishing other relationships and producing new meanings for children and adults with the world, with things and with life.

The cyborg metaphor gives us clues to understand that the cyborg itself, like technologies and gender, are human constructions. Therefore, if they are constructed, they can be denaturalized in the educommunicative process by choosing to be a Particle Physicist or a housewife, as Hari Kunzru (2016) problematizes.

Educommunication presupposes the presence of communicative ecosystems, a term used by Martin-Barbero (2014) to refer to different languages through technological and communicative environments made up of audiovisual languages. For this education and communication theorist, based on the premise of the existence of communicative ecosystems, it is essential that schools and the education system are concerned with the changes and alterations that society is undergoing, especially in the ways of teaching and learning mediated by the information and communication media.

From this point of view, communicative ecosystems in education need teachers who understand this reality of which they are a part and share the thinking of policies that value differences and overcome hierarchies and the dichotomous fractioning of gender issues. By using pedagogical practices concerned with equity when dealing with the subject of feminism, these education professionals can contribute to their own learning and that of their children in a critical and emancipatory way, like Haraway's (2009) metaphor of cyborgs.

It's important to note that the concept of communicative ecosystem was used in this text based on two authors. The first, Martin-Barbero (2014) describes communicative ecosystems in relation to the cultural changes caused by digital technologies within an educational environment of information and knowledge that is not limited to the knowledge acquired at school. The second, Ismar Soares (2014) thinks of Educommunication as a set of actions whose purpose is to integrate democratic, open and participatory communication processes into educational practices with the aim of creating and strengthening communicative ecosystems in educational spaces.

> The technological revolution we're experiencing doesn't just affect each medium individually, but produces transversal transformations that show the emergence of a communicative ecosystem shaped not only by new machines or media, but by new languages, writings and knowledge, by the hegemony of the audiovisual experience over the typographic one and the reintegration of the image into the field of knowledge production. This is having an impact both on the meaning and scope of what we mean by communication and also on the particular reallocation of each medium in this ecosystem and on the media's relationships with each other. (MARTIN-BARBERO, 2014, p.66)

From this perspective, the communicative ecosystem is understood as a space that enables the construction and reconstruction of collective, democratic and shared knowledge of pedagogical practices. In this movement, the exercise of teaching and learning in and with digital information and communication technologies takes place precisely in the transformation of information dispersed in cyberspace into meaningful knowledge, since it is "from the school that the dimensions, and not just the cultural effects of communicative technologies, must be thought about and taken on board" (MATIN-BARBERO, 2014, p.56).

> This set of new values characterizes a new world that is still in formation. A world in which the man-machine relationship is acquiring a new status, another dimension. Communication machines, computers, these new technologies, are no longer just machines. They are instruments of a new reason. In this sense,

machines cease to be, as they have been until now, an element of mediation between man and nature and come to express a new cognitive reason. (PRETTO, 2013, p.67)

Therefore, by understanding school education from the perspective of policies that foster this relationship between humans and non-humans and that refute the dichotomous performances of gender, a relational process emerges that offers possibilities for historical, social and cultural transformations, especially those focused on feminism. But how do we bring together these different elements that make up the communicative ecosystems - ICTs, feminist politics, children and teachers - and bring them into classroom practice?

In view of educommunicative pedagogical practices as an important way of establishing social relationships that respect differences and are based on a flat and symmetrical ontology, as Latour (2012) presents with the TAR, the stories of real women who have contributed in some way to reducing gender and power hierarchies seem to be a good didactic alternative. One of the educational strategies that can enhance the pedagogical dialogue with/on digital media in order to transform the instrumental view of these technologies into mediators of the teaching-learning process linked to feminist political movements could be the story of Malala Yousafzai. The Pakistani girl who was awarded the Nobel Peace Prize in 2014 for using digital information and communication technologies to demand the right of girls and women to study.

So, moving on to the next chapter, we'll talk a little more about Malala's story and what the links are with digital media to promote a society that claims rights within a feminist bias and with inspiration from the politics of cyborgs that Haraway (2009) inspires us with.

4 MALALA'S VOICE THROUGH DIGITAL MEDIA: THE RIGHT TO GO TO SCHOOL

"Who is Malala? Malala is me, and this is my story" (YOUSAFZAI, 2013, p.18).

We begin this text with a picture of Malala Yousafzai, a young Pakistani activist who was born in South Asia during the northern hemisphere's summer solstice at the end of the 20th century. Her name was inspired by the stories of the mountain people, the *Pashtuns*[3] , who fought against the British occupation of Afghanistan at the end of the 19th century.

> My name was chosen in honor of Malalai of Maiwand, the greatest heroine of Afghanistan. The Pashtuns are a proud people, made up of many tribes, divided between Pakistan and Afghanistan [...] The worst thing that can happen to a Pashtun is dishonor. [...] We have fought and fought so many endless eternal disputes that our word for cousin - *tarbur* - is the same as the one we use for enemy. But we always unite against outsiders who try to conquer our lands. All Pushtun children grow up hearing the story of how Malalai inspired the Afghan Army to defeat the British in the Second Anglo-Afghan War in 1880. (YOUSAFZAI, 2013, p.22)

[3] It is important to note that while Adriana Carranca's (2015) children's literature book names the Pashtun people, Malala Yousafzai's (2013) autobiography names the same people as Pashtuns. In the text, we have chosen to use both forms of writing.

Figure 5 - Pashtuns. Source: Carranca, 2015, p.10

Malala was named by her father after Malalai Maiwand, who joined the Pashtuns' struggle against the British occupation. Although Malalai was shot by British troops, her story has influenced and still motivates Afghans and the peoples of the surrounding area, including the Swat Valley in Pakistan (CARRANCA, 2015; YOUSAFZAI, 2013).

> Malalai was killed by the British, but her words and courage inspired the men [and women] to turn the battle around. They destroyed an entire brigade - one of the worst defeats in the history of the British Army. The Afghans built a monument to Maiwand's victory in the center of Kabul. Later, when I read some Sherlock Holmes books, I laughed to see that it was in this battle that Dr. Watson was wounded before becoming the great detective's partner. Malalai and the Pushtun Joan of Arc. Many girls' schools in Afghanistan are named after her. (YOUSAFZAI, 20013, p. 23)

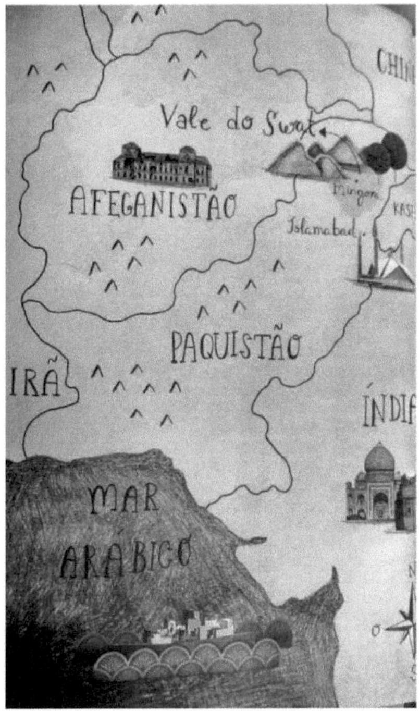

Figure 6 - Map of the Swat Valley. Source: Carranca, 2015, p.8

Malala, therefore, is known worldwide for being a human rights defender, especially for intervening for the right of women to attend school at a time when the Taliban - who took power in the Swat Valley - banned them from studying. Since then, Malala has become an activist with her voice heard by millions of people through her media reports. We therefore propose to consider how the media, especially digital media, can influence and contribute to social movements, especially the feminist movement and the human rights movement.

We won't be concerned with answering this question directly, , but rather with bringing to the center of the dialogue what Donna

Haraway (2009) has signaled to us through cyborgs: digital technologies as a power of transformation and change for 21st century society. To think that the cyborg is the very product of science and technology "the realities of modern life imply such an intimate relationship between people and technology that it is no longer possible to say where we end and where the machines begin." (KUNZRU, 2016, p.22). In other words, thinking about education as a way of denaturalizing gender expectations. In view of the above, we will continue the story of the young woman who won the Nobel Peace Prize in 2014 and how these technologies, as opposed to being used by conservative and oppressive initiatives, can help us strengthen an education for feminism.

During the Taliban takeover of the Swat Valley in 2009, Abdul Hai Kakar, a friend of Malala's father and a correspondent for the BBC (Brigith Broadcasting Corporation) in Peshwar (Pakistan), was looking for someone who could describe daily life under the Taliban regime. As an international news network, the BBC was keen to show what people in the Swat region experienced under the fundamentalist rule of the Taliban.

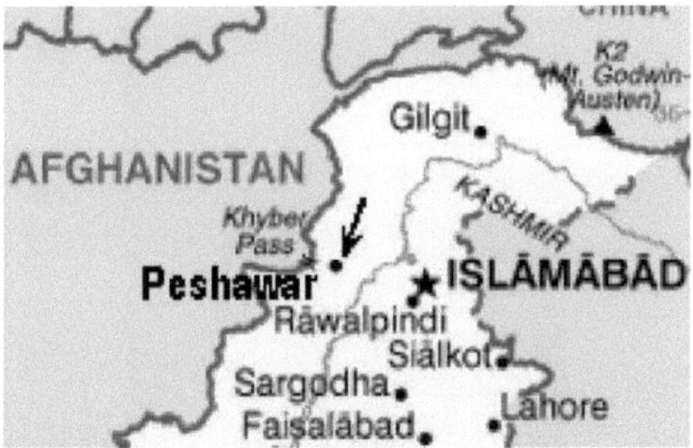

Figure 7 - Map of Pashwar (Pakistan) Source: Google Map

Both in the documentary directed by Davis Guggenheim (2015) and in the book (YOUSAFZAY, 2013), Malala set out to write this diary which she would present on the BBC's digital portal in Urdu. Even though she didn't know how or where to start, she believed it was important for people in other countries to know what was happening in the Swat Valley under Taliba control, led by Fazlullah.

I wanted people to know what was going on. Education is our right, I said. Just like it's our right to sing. Islam has given us this right by saying that every girl and boy must go to school. It is written in the Heart that we must seek knowledge, study hard and learn about the mysteries of our world. (YOUSAFZAI, 2013, p.164)

Malala began her denunciation process, sometimes in writing and sometimes by telephone.

The Taliban regime ordered the burning of books, the bombing of schools and the destruction of digital communication channels such as computers. There were frequent power cuts, so it wasn't always possible to write directly on the blog that would go to the BBC website.

His [Taliba] men blew up the power station and the valley was plunged into darkness. Battery-operated radios were the only entertainment. But all that could be heard was the voice of Fazlullah [...] It was on the radio that he sent news that the girls were forbidden to go to school. (CARRANCA, 2015, p.44)

Figure 8 - Malala documentary cover Source: Guggenheim (2015)

Figure 9 - Malala's book - autobiography Source: Yousafzai, 2013

Malala wrote under the pseudonym Gul Makai, under pain of being discovered by the Taliban and threatened with death. The media, especially digital media such as the BBC news, has undoubtedly been a partner in the struggle and claim for the rights of a people whose lives have been controlled by Fazluhllah's violent fundamentalism.

Gul Makai's blog was published in Urdu on the website of Britain's BBC radio and television network [...] Protected by anonymity, she continued to write. Her posts humanized the war. Everyone learned about the tragedy of Swat and the drama of the girls because of Malala's blog - that is, Gul Makai's blog. (CARRANCA, 2015, p. 47)

Gul Makai's diary was widely read and some newspapers even reproduced it. Malala came to understand that "the pen and words can be much more powerful than machine guns, tanks or helicopters. We were learning to fight. And realizing how powerful we are when we speak out." (YOUSAFZAI, 2013, p.167). With this, Malala achieved great popularity and she began to give interviews in the press and on television networks in various parts of the world.

Even after Malala's school was destroyed, she continued to write the blog. One day, she received a call from a student at Stanford University in the USA, originally from the capital of Pakistan, saying that she had watched the New York Times documentary - Forbidden Classes in the Swat Valley - and, in the words of Malala's own book, "Once again we see the power of magic" (YOUSAFZAI, 2013, p.173). This excerpt reminds us of the breadth and power that demands gain with digital technologies, as Donna Haraway (2009) warned us with the voice of the cyborgs.

Malala's struggle translates an entire nation of people, especially women, who do not have the right to study, who suffer successive forms of violence and who are victims of laws imposed by male chauvinist domination in different places around the world. The gender issues defended by theorists such as Donna Haraway (2009), Judith Butler (2003), Guacira Louro (2003), Joan Scott (1990), among many others, refute the hierarchical inequality between men and women.

The concept of gender was formulated with great influence from the feminist social movement in the 1970s. The concept is broad and follows different understandings and perspectives in which this work does not restrict itself to just one reductionist characteristic, however, one of the expressions adopted in general is precisely to deconstruct the idea that biological differences - vagina and penis, for example - because they do not justify the inequalities of rights between men and women.

> The very idea that a specific category is needed to analyze issues involving social hierarchies based on the ways in which each society gives meaning to the perceived differences between the sexes has a history. And that history can begin with the moment when women took to the streets to demand political rights and some other social rights, such as access to education and many careers that had been closed to them (WOLF; SILVA, 2015, p.96-97).

Although, according to some theorists, the category of gender emerged with the so-called second wave (some associate it with a third wave) of the feminist movement, after World War II, with demands for the right to the body and pleasure (PEDRO, 2015a), it was not present at the very beginning, in the 1960s and 1970s. Simone de Beauvoir (1970) - The Second Sex - in the 1950s - and Betty Friedan (1971) - Feminine Mystique - in the 1960s, although pioneers in the second-wave feminist movement, used the category woman in opposition to man. In other words, what was being questioned was the generalization and universalization of the masculine in our society. To illustrate this, we can first think of the Portuguese language. All beings, living or not, have gender, but not all of them have sex. This is why feminist women's movements in the 1980s began to use gender instead of sex (PEDRO, 2015b).

This summary does not reflect the complexity and struggles of women's groups over time. The movements did not happen in a simplistic and abrupt way as it might seem given the few words limited to a few lines and a single example transported into Portuguese. However, it should be borne in mind that these struggles for gender equality are called waves because of their similarity to sound and magnetic waves. It is an effect that is produced in all directions, continuously. By transposing this concept of waves to feminist movements, we can see that they go in different directions, such as black women, indigenous women, women agricultural workers.... In other words, the diversity and specificity of each group within a human rights perspective cannot be limited to a single category "woman", but rather to the plural, "women".

The category of women, consequently, arose with the demands of various feminist movements, such as the struggle of black women, indigenous women, rural workers, laborers... Since the category of "woman" (in which a different identity from that of man is constructed) was not enough to explain other women (rural, indigenous, black...). However, it must be emphasized that even with the differences between women, it is not possible to forget the inequalities produced in the power relations between the sexes (PEDRO, 2015b).

But beware, you need to pay attention to the historical process of the categories "woman" and "women". They are not presented on an evolutionary scale, since the category "woman" has been taken up by certain historians in order to recover the narrative of great women. In other words, the fact that historians use the category "women" does not exclude a vast production using the category "woman". According to Joana Pedro (2015b), the category "gender" emerged within the category "women", when writing the history of women. For her, gender is constructed in social relations based on the perceived differences between the sexes and built within power relations.

In view of the above, we need to think about education within schools. Gender-related issues within formal educational institutions imply preparing teachers to deal with everyday situations involving pupils, parents and the school staff.

It is important to discuss gender and education because the school institution, explicitly or implicitly, through its curriculum, its political pedagogical project, annual plan, lesson plans, teaching materials, pedagogical practices, languages, games, is still a privileged place for discussion and reflection on the production and reproduction of inequalities between genders. (GRAUPE; SOUZA, 2015, p.111)

Just as Malala defends the right of girls to go to school in the 21st century, we still have countless other cases of gender inequality and hierarchy. However, digital technologies can help us - and have helped us - to overcome this challenge, mobilizing issues related to school institutions and the media for feminism.

Malala's story doesn't end here. It is permeated by an attack that left her in a coma for several months, after she revealed her identity under the pseudonym Gul Makai. Contradictory to the story of Malalai of Maiwand, whose protagonist fought against the British, Malala went to live in England, where she still receives shelter and protection from the same country that once tried to dominate South Asia and the Pashtun people. There are many stories of exclusion, suffering and achievement. These stories can be told, lived and problematized by contemporary society in order to continue the fight for human rights and towards feminism, whether at school, at home or anywhere.

5 FINAL CONSIDERATIONS

The composition of this study was developed during the Gender and Diversity at School Specialization Course held at the Federal University of Santa Catarina between 2015 and 2016 and taught in various cities in the state. Several teachers and educators wrote and dialogued on topics involving feminism, diversity and human rights. Right from the start, I was assigned to class D - Donna Haraway. Without me knowing who I was, the universe seemed to have conspired to make me a member of this class, with this name and for this study.

Donna Haraway, therefore, means more than an epistemologist from the field of science and sociology, Donna Haraway is a hybrid mixture of humans and objects, the very cyborg that moves on the feminist waves. Like the author of the Cyborg Manifesto (HARAWAY, 2009), the "D" group is not bound by the limits of where the human being ends and technology begins. We are an integrated part of a flow of metamorphoses of thought and the development of notions of equality between genders that drive the transformations and (de)constructions that we are heterogeneous, diverse and articulated beings.

Scientific discoveries don't happen at random, they are somehow being investigated until they get somewhere (CHALMERS, 2015). I say this because it takes immersion in a specialization course dedicated to understanding gender and diversity issues to establish connections and reflect on these themes. The encounter with colleagues, teachers, videos, the internet, the moodle environment, texts, posters, school, prejudices, differences and hierarchies transforms us and becomes part of the tangle of ideas and understandings of our own lives as a denaturalization of determinisms.

Donna Haraway (2009), symbolizing the course class and the respected American theorist, integrates cyberculture and technoscience. The course, for example, takes place both on the digital platform, moodle, and in person. Haraway (2009) brings us into the discussion of cyborgs at the frontiers, or rather, the dissolution of the frontiers of gender and technology.

Other authors refute the dichotomy of nature/society, science/pseudo-science, fact/myth, human/non-human, such as Bruno Latour (2012). Like Haraway (2012), he provokes us to think about networked relationships and not the separation of subject and object. After all, we are made up of hybrid elements and we make them up too. Like the process of formation throughout the course, we change our way of thinking and acting at the same time as we influence people, laws, decisions and actions.

The choice of children's literature in the figure of Pakistani Malala Yousafzai, winner of the 2014 Nobel Prize for demanding the right of women to go to school after the Taliba takeover of South Asian regions, was not random, as is often thought of with regard to scientific discoveries (CHALMERS, 2015). It was an attentive and careful choice for the visibility of a non-white, non-Western girl who used digital social networks to denounce the atrocities and abuses that fundamentalists in the name of religion imposed on the population, especially the women of her country. Malala, under the pseudonym Gui Makai, was able to communicate worldwide through the press (BBC) and mobilized people to fight the inequalities that were taking place.

Far from wanting to adopt a technocratic populist stance categorized as **promethean** by Francisco Rudiger (2013), in which technology occupies a privileged space restricted to the advances that social movements, especially those achieved by feminists, have made, in this work we seek to sustain the optimistic view of digital social media in its possibilities. However, it is necessary to make a brief reservation about a less encouraging view in which digital media navigate a two-way street in the movement of permissiveness, persecution and violence represented, for example, in the circulation of child images among pedophiles, in crimes against women and against any arguments in favor of feminism exposed mainly on social networks. With this, we don't intend to be silent about the problems that grow along with the advances, they exist and must be denounced. As an alternative to these more critical debates, we have chosen to give greater visibility to the possibilities that digital technologies can promote by encouraging other people to enter these paths of struggle and resistance against any trace of heteronormativity, sexism and trans-homophobia.

This relationship between information and communication technologies, in this case the BBC newspaper, and feminist awareness of the struggle for human rights reinforces Haraway's (2009) theory about cyborgs, while at the same time working with the possibilities of education. The children's literature book represents a playful way of understanding diversity, respect, mobilization and feminism, in order to help reduce gender hierarchies.

It is important to remember that "gender inequality" is not the same as "gender inequality". The latter refers to a substitution of gender in place of sex, in other words, a binary and dichotomous relationship from which we have tried to distance ourselves throughout the text, supported by authors and theorists in the field.

Malala's importance, therefore, is not restricted to her fight for feminism, but for breaking boundaries of age, for being a girl; gender, for being a woman; geography, for not being Western; and religion, for being a Muslim and criticizing the religious fundamentalism of Islam. It is through this bias that this work sought to problematize: diversity of thought as respect for values and not as a cultural, social or gender hierarchy.

In view of the above, it is worth finally reflecting briefly on the potential of the study of gender and diversity issues worked on throughout the course for education, not only as an educational institution, but in the family, in meetings with friends, at home, in public spaces and in critical reading. After all, education doesn't have a wall. The border is not the school. The digital means of information and communication are set in cyberculture. We are both receivers and producers of this media and we have to be aware of this movement in order to influence and bring to the dialog themes that address human rights, feminism and respect for differences, whatever they may be. There will be gender and diversity at school, YES!!!!!

REFERENCES

BASTOS, Rodolpho Alexandre Santos; NOGUEIRA Joanna Ribeiro. Gender stereotypes in fairy tales: a historical-pedagogical approach In: **Dimensoes**, v. 36, jan.-jun. 2016. Available at< file:///C:/Users/User/Downloads/13864-37254-1-SM.pdf> Accessed on 25 Aug 2016

BEAUVIOR, Simone de. **The second sex**: facts and myths. Vol. 1 Rio de Janeiro: Nova Fronteira, 1970.

BUTLER, Judith. **Gender trouble:** feminism and the subversion of identity. Rio de Janeiro: Brazilian Civilization, 2003

CARRANCA, Adriana. **Malala, the girl who wanted to go to school**. Sao Paulo: Companhia das Letrinhas, 2015.

CHALMERS, Alan. **What is science anyway**? Sao Paulo: Brasiliense, 2015

FRIEDAN, Betty. **The feminine mystique**. Petropolis: Vozes, 1971.

GRAUPE, Mareli Eliane; SOUSA, Lucia Aulete Burigo da. Gender and education. Discipline V. In: GROSSI, Miriam Pillar et al (org). **Gender and Diversity at School**. Book 2, module 2. Florianopolis: Institute of Gender Studies. Center for Philosophy and Human Sciences, UFSC, 2015.

GUGGENHEIM, Davis (director). **Malala.** Original title: He named me Malala. Documentary genre, 1h27min. USA, 2015

HARAWAY, Donna. Cyborg Manifesto. Science, technology and socialist-feminism at the end of the 20th century. In: HARAWAY, D.; KUNZRU, H.; TADEU, T. **Anthropologia do ciborgue: as vertigens do pos-humano**. Belo Horizonte: Autentica, 2009.

HJARVARD, Stig. **From Media to Mediaization**: the institutionalization of new media. Paragrafo Magazine, Jul/Dec 2015. Available at <http: //www.revistaseletronicas.fiamfaam. br/index.php/recicofi/article/view/331/339> Accessed on 13 Jun 2016.

Midiatización: theorizing the media as an agent of social and cultural change. Sao Paulo, Brazil: **Revista Matrizes ECA/USP** Ano 5 - n° 2 jan./jun. 2012. Available at<
http://www.matrizes.usp.br/index.php/matrizes/article/view/338/pdf> Accessed on 10 Jun 2016.

KERCKHOVE, Derrick de. **The skin of culture**. Sao Paulo: Annablume, 2009.

KIRCHOF, Edgar Roberto; BONIN, lara Tatiana; SILVEIRA, Rosa Maria Hessel. Introducing children's literature and differences. **Educagao & Realidade**, Porto Alegre, v. 38, n. 4, p. 1045-1052, Dec. 2013 . Available at:<
http://www.scielo.br/scielo.php?script=sci_arttext&pid=S2175-j62362013000400002&lng=en&nrm=iso> Accessed on 30 Jul 2016

KUNZRU, Hari. You are a cyborg: an encounter with Donna Haraway. In: **The vertigo of the posthuman**. SILVA, Tomaz Tadeu da (org). Belo Horizonte: Autentica Editora, 2016.

LATOUR, Bruno. **Reaggregating the social**: an introduction to Actor-Network Theory. Salvador: Edufba, 2012.

LOURO, Guacira Lopes. Curriculum, gender and sexuality - the "normal", the "different" and the "eccentric". In: LOURO, Guacira Lopes; GOELLNER, Silvana Vilodre.; NECKEL, Jane Felipe (Orgs.). **Body, gender and sexuality**. A contemporary debate in education. Petropolis: Vozes, 2003.

MARTIN-BARBERO, Jesus. **Communication in education**. Sao Paulo: Contexto, 2014.

MARTINO, Luis de Sa. **Teoria das Midias Digitais**: linguagens, ambientes, redes. Petropolis, RJ: Vozes, 2015.

PEDRO, Joana Maria. **The history of feminisms**. In: Cycle of Video Classes The History of Feminism GDE 2012-2013. Gender and Diversity at School, 2015 a.

PEDRO, Joana Maria. Translating the debate: the use of the gender category in historical research. Discipline III. In: GROSSI, Miriam Pillar et al (org). **Gender and Diversity at School**. Book 1, module 1. Florianopolis: Institute of Gender Studies. Center for Philosophy and Human Sciences, UFSC, 2015b.

PRETTO, Nelson. **A school with/without a future:** education and multimedia. Salvador: Edufba, 2013.

ROVELLI, Carlo. **Seven brief links to physics**. Rio de Janeiro: Objetiva, 2015.

RUDIGER, Francisco. **Theories of cyberculture**: perspectives, issues and authors. Porto Alegre: Sulina, 2013.

SARTORI,Ademilde (org).**Educommunication and the creation of communicative ecosystems**: dialogs without borders. Florianopolis: DIOESC, 2014

SCOTT, Joan. **Gender:** a useful category for historical analysis. Education and Reality, Porto Alegre. 1990.

SOARES, Ismar. **Educommunication**: the concept, the professional and the application. Sao Paulo: Editora Paulinas, 2014.

WOLF, Cristina Sheibe; SILVA, Janine Gomes da. **Gender:** an important concept for understanding the social world. Discipline III. In: GROSSI, Miriam Pillar et al (org). Gender and Diversity at School. Book 1, module 1. Florianopolis: Institute of Gender Studies. Center for Philosophy and Human Sciences, UFSC, 2015.

Printed by Books on Demand GmbH, Norderstedt / Germany